The 100

For Kickass Women Entrepreneurs Ready to Suck it Up and Finally Play Big

International Amazon Best-Selling Author Katrina Ruth

(formerly Kat Loterzo)

Published by: Katrina Ruth Pty Ltd

Edited by: Deanna Shanti – Shanti Publishing

Copyright © 2014 Katrina Ruth

www.thekatrinaruthshow.com

ISBN: 978-1-950212-01-9

Each month I like to give away courses or books! Receive your FREE 8 Day Video Training Series on The Truth About Successful Manifestation and join my online community of KICKASS women entrepreneurs at:

www.thekatrinaruthshow.com/manifestationfreecourse

For more kickass books for kickass women, including free downloads:

www.booksforkickasswomen.com

Table of Contents

INTRODUCTION

Time to wake the fuck up sister:

If you picked up this book, there are two things I know for sure about you-

1. You want it all

2. You want it now (if not sooner)

The truth about YOU is you dream bigger than anybody around you, you're the one everybody already calls superwoman, you take on more in a week than 10 normal woman would in a year, and you seriously do NOT get how everybody else is so slow and unmotivated in their lives.

What's wrong with them?! Surely they want more, surely they want BIGGER? You don't get it. But either way-

You are here to go ALL out, to spin the world on its heels and then dance on top all the while proclaiming your status as a best-selling author, internationally acclaimed speaker, thought leader and game-changer, and multi-million dollar PLUS business owner.

With the hair and wardrobe to match :)

Only thing is -

You're not.

You haven't.

And you don't QUITE have the income to match. (Or, frustratingly, the reach.)

But here's what else I know about you.

You're determined.

You do NOT let resistance or FEAR or stupid old EMOTIONS dictate your destiny.

You are in this for the long haul and the only time you STOP taking action on this journey will be when you stop LIVING.

Because to you? This FIGHT, this PUSH, this CONSTANT need for more?

That's living baby.

And you'll do whatever it takes -

For as long as it takes -

To get to where you want to go.

So here's what I want to tell you about me, and about this book -

I get it.

I feel your dreams.

I feel how big they are.

I KNOW you've got what it takes.

I believe in your destiny and your RIGHT to change the world and live completely on your terms.

And I can tell you from personal experience, after years of being that woman battling to create her business and life the way she'd always wanted it -

You really can have whatever you want.

Let's talk about how!

CHAPTER ONE - IT'S NOT ABOUT THE NUMBER

The title of this book? It's just a number, okay? I chose it because right now, as I write this, I've just started to consistently hit 100k (plus!) months in my online business.

Pretty cool :)

But also - whatever, right? By the time you read this I plan to be doing 200k months, 500k, maybe a million. The hits are just gonna keep on coming now that I've figured out this whole 'how to make money and live the life you want' thing.

Arrogant?

You can bet your ass I'll be arrogant about what I'm capable of, what I intend to make happen and WILL see happen, what I dream of for myself and then go out and get.

AND SO SHOULD YOU BE.

If you're NOT dreaming 100x bigger than ANYBODY else in your life, you're in the wrong place here beautiful.

Like I said -

You CAN have it all, you can have it all on YOUR terms, and you can have it all NOW.

But here's what they don't usually tell you in success school -

You want it all? You better get off your butt and go on out and GET it all sister, because the fact that you were born for something?

Doesn't mean you're going to get it.

YOU want it then YOU do the work and YOU make it happen. Day in and day out, ad infinitum.

In some ways, that's all you need to know about success. Of course, where the real work comes in is not, as you might think, so much in figuring out your plan or your HOW to do it all but rather, as you might secretly suspect, in dealing with the biggest demon you'll have to slay to enable you to actually DO that daily work, and do it all out.

You.

YOU are the one who will determine your success and you are ALSO the one most likely to fuck it all up.

If, for example, you allow fear to rule you.

Or you decide whether or not to do the work today based on how you FEEL.

Or you play into what other people THINK or EXPECT of you.

Or you filter how you say things 'cause hey! You gotta have people LIKE you, right?

The way that most of the world, and CERTAINLY the woman entrepreneur world plays for success is just so much bullshit.

Please like me!

Please like my pretty website!

Please let me play in the sandbox too!

Let's all have a hug!

Let's talk about our problems!

Let's WORK on ourselves!

Let's figure ourselves OUT!

Let's DISCUSS what we should be doing or could be doing instead of just freaking well DOING!

Let's get things PERFECT!

Let's have a meltdown and a massive group intervention whenever anybody questions our work, our thoughts, who we are.

Let's criticise or judge those who speak out loud and proud about their income, or their CRAZY big goals, or the fact that they don't care what the RULES are.

No, ladies. Not on my watch :)

You want this, you REALLY want it? You're going to have to cause some upset and stop caring about it. Matter of fact, you're going to have to WANT to cause some upset! Be honest now-

Don't you sometimes think that these people need to wake the fuck up?

It's like everybody around you is just floating through water.

Don't they CARE? Aren't they BRAVE? Aren't they willing to DO WHAT IT TAKES?

No.

They're not.

You are the 1% within the 1% in terms of the level at which you think and the speed at which you can take EFFECTIVE action.

So get used to doing more, being more and having more. That's what you want, right?

Time to start acting like it.

Oh, and the numbers thing? Listen up, because this is CRITICAL. Stop focusing on the number you want. Stop saying you want to make a million dollars, or 'x' amount per month or that you're next launch has to have these numbers. Stop focusing on an arbitrary number and instead get clear on what those numbers REPRESENT, and focus on bringing that into your life. You do that, and you can have any number you choose ;)

talk in IG about this concept

CHAPTER TWO - THE 100 MILLION DOLLAR QUESTION

I've said it before, and I'll say it again.

You dream bigger than big. You're ALREADY the superwoman. You're ALREADY the crazy high achiever. And if you're really honest, it's kind of BORING. What you need, is a real challenge.

What you need, is to start actually allowing in your TRUE goals right now.

What you need, quite simply, is to stop being such a pussy about what you're aiming for and for once be God damned HONEST about what it is you really see in your future.

I'm not going to judge you for wanting it all...

But if you're going to be able to go on out and GET it all then you might need to stop judging yourself...

And it MIGHT help to actually start regularly STATING what it is you really want...

Instead of pretending you're happy with this step-by-step, linear, slow-going, MIND-NUMBING process you currently have going on.

You want to know why you haven't yet achieved ALL your goals, and then some? It's because you're so busy focusing on where you are now and what you need to do 'next'!

Let's flip that situation around.

Imagine -

You're there.

You have it all.

You're doing it all.

And then some.

How does it look gorgeous?

How does it REALLY look?

The 100 Million Dollar Question is one I ask of myself and my clients anytime I think we've stepped back into the (UGH!) realistic zone.

It's pretty freaking simple.

And pretty freaking powerful.

If you had a 100 million dollars in the bank, right now, who would you choose to be and what would you choose to be doing?

How would you spend your time?

What would you put out into the world?

Who would you work with?

Who would you NOT work with and what else would you let go of?

Who would you be WITHIN yourself?

What would you be DOING for yourself?

Where would you live?

With who?

And what else?

What EVERYTHING else?

We're talking about (finally!) painting the picture for your true ultimate business and life.

You know that thing you do, where you think about what you want to create for yourself, for your business, for your life? Where you imagine yourself hitting those goals, making that money, buying that cool stuff, taking those trips?

Go bigger.

Go ALL the way.

Go RIGHT into the deepest darkest recesses of your mind into where you don't usually dare to even LOOK. And tell me -

What's the real dream, hmmm?

What's the dream so big it scares the living PANTS off of you?

What's the dream that makes you feel crazy, foolish, reckless, naive, or even EMBARRASSED?

What do you REALLY want and what is your IMPOSSIBLE DREAM that we're now going to make possible?

Funny thing about setting goals and bringing them into life. If you believe in ANY form in the law of attraction, in creating your own reality, in your ability to choose and to live life on your terms, then it MEANS THAT YOU BELIEVE.

There's no grey area here. You either believe, or you don't believe.

If you don't believe, leave.

Seriously, you're wasting your time here and I am NOT writing to you.

But if you believe? Then you fucking well believe!

Which means...

If you think about it...

That the fact that you're asking for ANYTHING less than what it is you REALLY want...

Is just kind of STUPID.

I mean, if a fairy Godmother came up and told you that you could have ANYTHING in the world and that having it would NOT in any way take it away from anybody else in the world; that it would in fact allow others more as more begets more, then would you ask for a few pennies and a pat on the back, or would you ASK FOR WHAT YOU REALLY WANT?

The only reason you don't yet HAVE it all is that you haven't CHOSEN to have it all. Asking for less, CHOOSING less, doesn't get you any points in heaven gorgeous. It's all there for the taking anyway ... it's like oxygen ... you can breathe shallow if you really WANT to, but why would you? Just seems kinda foolish when taking nice BIG breaths is going to feel so much better and make life so much easier.

So, a few reminders for you, because I know it's sometimes hard to get your head around this stuff:

If you make a hundred million dollars, it doesn't mean anybody ELSE missed out.

It doesn't make you a bad person.

It doesn't mean you're greedy -

Or selfish -

Or that you're plain old chasing something you don't need -

IT JUST MEANS YOU WERE WILLING TO ALLOW IT IN.

And that's the thing, isn't it? You're not going to GET anything you didn't decide to ALLOW.

So if right now you're telling yourself you in ANY way have to wait to realise your true dreams … or that you shouldn't aim THAT big … or that it's not that easy …

Then guess what?

You'll get exactly what you expect.

But only 100% of the time ;)

So here's a little challenge for ya, if you dare -

Decide.

Right now.

Yes, this very moment!

That you?

Are nobody's bitch baby and ESPECIALLY not the world's. You've got shit to DO, a calling to live out, and a DAMN fine life to live.

But if you WANT it you know you gotta go on out and TAKE it. So before you move on to the next chapter, get your pen and paper out and write yourself your TRUE dreams for this business, and this life. And don't be afraid to DREAM LIKE YOUR LIFE ACTUALLY DEPENDS UPON IT.

Ain't nobody gonna press play for you beautiful.

do an IG, talk about this

CHAPTER THREE - AMBITION IS NOT A DIRTY WORD - FUCK THE NAYSAYERS!

Did you ever have the feeling that other people think badly of you for wanting a life of more, and for seeing yourself as somebody capable of achieving more?

Honestly, if you ask ME, and I know that you haven't but this is my book so I'm gonna go ahead and say it anyway, the way that most of the world thinks about success, and life, is complete and utter bullshit!

I mean seriously ... get a house, a mortgage, a job and then the next job? Take a trip once or twice a YEAR and to somewhere 'nice' that you can 'afford'? Delay living your dreams and life on your terms for 40 freaking years until you're retired or DEAD?

Utter, utter BS, not to mention the fact that it's downright CRIMINAL to try and impose such limited thinking onto others around you.

But yet, that is what the world at large does, isn't it?

Tells you -

This is what is normal to aim for.

This is how it works.

Here is what to expect.

Here is what you must do.

And here's how you must be in order to achieve all of that.

I mean seriously ... if you were standing on the outside looking IN to the way that the human race lives wouldn't you just think it was a race of pre-programmed bots of some kind? Drones, destined to an existence of mediocrity because hey! Wouldn't want to stir the pot! Wouldn't want to colour outside the lives. Wouldn't want to (gasp!) THINK FOR YOURSELF NOW WOULD YOU?!

And I don't know about you, but personally when I look at the way people just lemming-like fall into line with this shit, I gotta tell you -

I'm not buying it.

I don't BELIEVE that they are happy, satisfied, fulfilled, or in flow when the quests that they embark upon to achieve these things are quests dictated to and then watched over by those who have gone before them, and are going alongside of them.

exactly!

The worst part is - I think that they are FULLY AWARE OF THIS and yet they continue to PERPETUATE the problem, encouraging their friends, families and loved ones to be realistic, to settle down, to get a good job, to stay the course because hey! You've come this far.

Of course ultimately it's not up to either you or me to dictate how others should live ... if they want to march on off that cliff into oblivion with the rest of the race then we can't really stop 'em. At least not directly. But where it impacts upon YOU and where it becomes not only your right but your RESPONSIBILITY to do something about it is when it is influencing how you live YOUR life.

Tell me now, and be honest. Have you ever found yourself in ANY way turning away from your soul's deepest desires because you had to be realistic? Because you had your family to think of? Because it might not WORK, and so what's the point? Because you didn't know how? Or simply because something inside of you (it's a chip, they put it there!) was telling you that no! You can't have a life like that, you can't just live any old way, you have to do it THIS way.

If you answered yes even once then guess what?

You've been tainted with the naysayer brush. On the odd occasion, this is not an awful thing and it's pretty much unavoidable completely, but when you start to LISTEN and it starts to become a habit and then a way of thinking that turns into a way of LIVING?

We got problems sister.

ESPECIALLY when you consider that if you look to those around you for empowering support, inspiration and motivation what you are likely to receive instead is a nice old shove back into your box.

Where it's cosy...

Safe...

Comfortable...

You can fit in...

Nobody will question you...

And you can (pretend to) happily eke out the rest of your days as one of THEM.

If you're REALLY good at deluding yourself you might even convince yourself that this is how it has to be, really.

That those dreams and fantasies were just that-fantasies.

Not for this life.

Which means not for ever.

The only thing is...

You know better.

Don't'cha?

You're not actually CAPABLE of fully conforming, even though at times you might consider it because it would just be EASIER.

In my previous relationship, when a fight would ensue, one of my partner's 'go-to' taunts was that I held myself in higher regard than those around me, including, I suppose the implication was, him.

He would sneer at me in the third person, saying things like -

"Katrina thinks she's the Queen... Katrina's so much better than everyone else ... oh Katrina can do whatever she likes because she ALWAYS knows best and is never wrong!"

The thing is, I've never feel I am BETTER than anyone else, not if by better you mean better on a fundamental level.

However I know, and it's not arrogance or pride that causes me to say this but simply KNOWING, that I am better at taking action than some.

That I am better at committing whole-heartedly to my dreams and goals.

And that I am better or at least BIGGER in the way I dream them in the first place.

For him, as much as he, in calm moments, professed to support and be proud of me, the stuff that came out when things got heated always seemed to me to have an undercurrent of fury. Fury that I thought I could just live life however I like, that I could just have whatever I set my mind on. Fury, I suppose, because who the hell did I think I was?

I couldn't stand the way he would put words into my mouth about what I supposedly thought about myself - I sure as heck knew I wasn't perfect and professed it often - but mostly I found it FRUSTRATING because so what if I dreamed bigger than big? So what if I was willing to put aside society's rules and obligations so that I could create my life on my terms.

I guess in the end the truth about that relationship was that me chasing MY dreams and heart in some way stopped him having a life that felt right to him.

The really fucked up thing here is that he saw my desire to want MORE and my choice to be confident in my abilities, as a character flaw. It's not like you throw the things you love about someone at them as insults during a fight, is it?

Are you with me here? How crazy is it to hate on someone for having big dreams and goals, and for choosing the self-belief and confidence necessary to create those big dreams and goals?

I think it's freaking ridiculous!

Just like he thought that it was ME who was freaking ridiculous.

So here's the thing about that, and this is a tough one -

I don't believe it's possible for you to ever sustain a DEEP relationship of ANY kind with someone who has such fundamentally different beliefs about how life works, and how we should all act. You can have a fair crack at it ... convince yourself that it doesn't matter so much, that you can talk with your entrepreneur buddies about this stuff, but the truth is that the lemming-like people? As much as you might like or even love them, they will bore you.

And you will PERPETUALLY infuriate them with your drive.

It's a recipe doomed for frustration, with the only exception being if deep down YOU truly want to conform and are looking to be 'safely' pulled back in (if so, leave this book RIGHT NOW - NOT for you!) or alternatively if THEY have undercurrents of wanting more that they're looking to unleash. Sometimes, with time, you might find you've influenced someone enough to pull them back out of their zombie-like state and into actually waking up and thinking the fuck about how they want their life to be. But in the meantime, if you choose to keep hanging around these people, you're also choosing to open yourself up to up close and personal judgment of who you ARE.

Which is pretty messed up.

I know for me, in that relationship, even when we weren't fighting, there was often tension around the fact that I LIKED to work. Anger when I would spend time on it in lieu of other things. And a general frustration at my incessant drive, the fact that I was never done, never truly satisfied, never really happy to rest because when I WAS happy was when I was creating and getting my message out there.

To me this is mind boggling - the idea that my ambition could be considered a bad thing. At times I would question - am I working too much? Do I talk about work all the time? Is it all I care about? Do I think too highly of myself? Depending upon the situation you could argue in either direction for all cases, but ultimately what it comes down to is that we all want different things and we all have a different sort of drive.

It's not right, or wrong.

It just is.

So here's what I want you to know today.

A couple of things.

Firstly - AMBITION is not a dirty word.

It's okay to want more.

It's okay to want it all.

And it's okay to choose to believe in yourself enough to go on out and TAKE it all.

Secondly.

You're not alone. There are others who think AS BIG AS YOU DO. I used to think that I dreamt bigger than anybody else I KNEW. And then I joined a mastermind where people were working on building $100 million dollar businesses. Why? BECAUSE THEY COULD. Amongst other reasons, but that was one of 'em! It blew my mind. For many people, the concept of aiming that big ANGERS them, like why SHOULD you? It's greedy / selfish / not necessary and so many other blah di blah thoughts which I'm sure you can fill in for yourself.

So yes.

There are OTHERS JUST LIKE YOU.

Which brings me to my third point -

It is not just a good idea to actively cultivate an environment for yourself that spurs you faster to your dreams it is ESSENTIAL.

I spent years creating my dream life and business with the wrong person by my side, and while I still moved forward and even influenced him to think bigger to a degree, ultimately it was a HUGE energy drain and source of stress. For both of us, not just for me! Because no matter which way I tried to spin it - we weren't in alignment from a values standpoint. On other issues as well, but this was certainly a big one.

So when I said, in the title of this chapter, that you should fuck the naysayers, I'm not just saying it to write an in your face chapter title. I'm saying it because you need to FUCK THE NAYSAYERS.

Fuck 'em on right out of your life.

YES it is harsh and YES the world will judge you for it, call you cold or uncaring or relentlessly driven (thank you!), and YES you COULD, or in many people's minds, SHOULD put the feelings and beliefs of others first but really?

Do you want to put ANYBODY else's beliefs about life, about YOUR life specifically, ahead of your own?

Ambition is NOT a dirty word gorgeous.

You DO have a purpose.

I KNOW you've got a calling.

There IS a reason you're here.

And you ARE meant for more.

But if you want to truly live at THAT level? Then it is your DUTY to protect and actively daily CHOOSE what comes into your mind, because you're sure as heck not gonna have something come out different to what went in.

Time to dream big lady!

And then go out and claim it.

Life is now, you know? Better press play ;)

CHAPTER FOUR - YOU ALREADY CHOSE

I'm going to say this once, and once only.

Just before we get into the stuff of ACTION taking, and making this shit HAPPEN.

The life you have right now? Is exactly the one you asked for. So as we look at how you can go BIGGER, know this -

Whatever your excuses, your reasons, your absolutely TRUE justifications as to why you can't do it that way, not yet, not YOU, know this -

I've heard 'em all.

Mostly from me.

And I ain't buying it.

You WANT it? THEN YOU FREAKING WELL TAKE IT. And you do NOT take no for an answer, not from anybody and sure as HECK not from yourself.

YOU GET WHAT YOU CHOOSE, so if you don't LIKE what you've chosen then for fuck's sake choose something else!

We clear?

CHAPTER FIVE - THE MOST IMPORTANT ACTION YOU CAN TAKE TO REACH YOUR DREAMS

Okay, so this? Is where the rubber starts to hit the road gorgeous. Because if you want to see this stuff HAPPEN? You're kind of going to have to make it happen.

And before we jump into it, let's get one thing straight -

When I say you're going to have to MAKE it happen? YOU'RE GOING TO HAVE TO MAKE IT HAPPEN.

Like, consistently.

Daily.

Forever.

I'm guessing you probably KNOW this, but do you KNOW IT AND LIVE IT?

For me, back in 2007, when I first started writing online, I'd never really heard of the idea of running a business online. My big plan was simply to, in some way, increase business as a Personal Trainer in my home-town of Melbourne, and I also wanted to use and better my skills as a writer.

I figured that having an 'online newsletter' of sorts would be a good way to get the word out more, maybe help position me at the top of my industry and mean I could get some cool new gigs like corporate fitness work and in-house speaking for local companies.

Which it did.

But also -

You know how once you get an idea into your head and start to imagine if maybe - just MAYBE - it might also be POSSIBLE (for you!), you just can't seem to let go of that thing?

I don't know where I first really 'got' the possibility of making money online; I think it probably just crept up on me, but at some point I realised -

Oh shit! This blogging thing is just the beginning!

I can write EBOOKS...!

And SELL them...!

Maybe even get PAID TO WRITE...!

And coach people online ... somehow!

It all sounded very mysterious and exciting and a little scary but any 'how do I' fears were fears I chose to ignore, and instead I started to look for proof that all of this stuff was possible.

(Hint: one of the fastest and most sure-fire ways, I've found, to catapult you to your crazy 'how do I' dreams, is to actively hunt for proof it's possible. Get your hands and eyes on as many case studies and transformations as you can, because if THEY can do it then so too can you! Not to mention that the default is everybody and their dog telling you to be more realistic - yawn!)

I read blogs like Problogger and Copyblogger daily, and I was a big fan of Yaro Starak who spoke about how he lived his 'laptop life' and could work from anywhere in the world - was in fact doing so! - with just his laptop and an internet connection, and make a full time living.

It sounded AMAZING.

Too good to be true...

Overwhelming to figure out...

And abso-freaking-LUTELY what I knew I WOULD somehow figure out and make happen.

'Cause if this shit was possible? No way was I going to miss out on joining the party!

So I got to work.

I blogged and guest posted and read and commented and even joined Facebook after a year or so! I spent 26 months crafting my first eBook after obsessively learning what I thought was the path to a million dollars via eBooks from Alexis Dawes, and I made precisely $411 on my launch day.

I was STOKED, because it proved everything I'd been working so hard for, and I knew -

If I could make $1 online, I could make $1000, $10,000, $100,000, and then some.

Fast forward to now, and in total I've made somewhere in the region of 1.5 - 2 million dollars online. Ask me again a year from now and it will be over 10 million total assuming I hit my next 12 month commitments. Which I certainly am committed to, having recently upgraded my New Year income goal to 10 mil plus for the calendar year ... aiming for the stars baby!

Only thing was at the time and back when that ball FIRST started rolling ... 3 years after I wanted it to start rolling and first tried to get it to...

It was kind of hard going!

After 3 years online I'd made maybe $10,000 total from my efforts, and I'd put in up to 40 hours a week on top of already working full-time as a personal trainer. I'd gone through my first pregnancy, gone back to part-time personal training, had some cool experiences through my blog (a stand out was when one of the people I most revered at the time as a writer, Sarah Wilson, contacted ME out of the blue to tell me how much she loved my writing for Dumb Little Man, a site I often guested on!), and I certainly enjoyed the whole thing but it was also, to be honest, just a lot of work. It was definitely making it easy for me to have an endless stream of face to face clients as my positioning in Melbourne and even Australia for my niche was pretty high on Google, but where was this laptop life I'd been dreaming of?

I wanted MORE!

I wanted all of it!

And I wanted it now.

But as much as I fought it, I couldn't help wondering -

What am I doing wrong?

What am I missing here?

Why aren't I EXPLODING online?

Why doesn't everyone know who I am yet?!

Why aren't I famous and rich?!

I have to be honest, I have never questioned whether or not I will 'make it'. I've come close, but my underlying and firmly held belief has always been that I'll be a wildly successful, wealthy entrepreneur, live life exactly as I please and be famed internationally as a transformative author and speaker.

But in 2010, when I'd been plugging away for so long and really my efforts over a 3-year period online were nothing to write home about AND they were starting to irritate my husband with how much of me they consumed, it was very, very tempting to put myself on some kind of 'just had a baby and this whole blogging thing sucks and isn't really working anyway' hiatus.

But for some reason, somehow, and despite often getting frustrated or tired of the whole process and despite frequently questioning my own sanity and my WHY, when it would have been so much easier (and more 'normal' as a new Mum!) to spend any free time (ha!) or baby nap time resting, I kept going.

Every day, I rocked my little daughter off to sleep in her stroller, and I made my way to a local cafe, for an hour if I could be so lucky, 40 minutes or so was normal, and occasionally there'd be those tormenting times when she'd wake within minutes or refuse to go down at all and I'd be there with a bottle of expressed milk in one hand (if I was organised, if not then a boob out and a baby on my lap!) and I'd type with as many fingers and as much speed possible.

And I'd read something that inspired me.

And I'd journal and dream.

And then I'd write.

What would I write?

Anything. Everything. Something.

A blog, an idea, a dream. Notes for books that for years never came to life, some which still have not. New online course and product ideas, some of which I even brought to life.

And a lot of big plans and visions.

I didn't have a lot of structure. I didn't have any themes for my blog posts and online newsletters. I didn't have a publishing schedule to stick to. I didn't always take action on all my big dreams and goals. In a lot of ways you could say I wasted a lot of time.

I didn't really know WHAT I was working for, or towards, when nobody was 'making me' and perhaps not many people would have even noticed if I stopped, but for whatever reason I just. Kept. Going.

Have you ever had a calling within you, deep and dark and mysterious, and freaking FRUSTRATING because you know it's there, you feel it there, you can't escape or avoid it and yet you also can't manage to put your finger on it?

I knew I was meant for more...

I knew I was going to go big...

I knew I was going to go ALL the way!

But I just couldn't figure out how to bring that big, big dream and vision into the here and now. How could I, when I couldn't even fully define what I wanted to do or be known for?!

You know?

But most of the time, I didn't really stop to try and figure it out. Oh sure, I wrote about it (in my private journal, and sometimes publically) and I questioned it and I sure did a lot of coaching and personal development and read EVERYTHING I could get my hands on along the lines of passion and purpose and working from a place of truth and flow, but mostly?

I just. Kept. Going.

I dreamed my big dreams and then I took action on them. Unquestionably it was imperfect and mostly completely naive action, and a high percentage of the time it was action that probably had nothing at all to do with DIRECTLY helping me achieve the money, the fame, the reach, the transformation I desire, but be that as it may it was ACTION.

And action drives you forward.

I don't know if you've ever found yourself wondering, as I so often did, what you're missing.

What does everyone else know that you don't?

Why does their STUFF always seem better ... glossier ... more exciting ... more RIGHT...?

Why are you STILL feeling 'stuck'?

Why isn't your list growing as fast as you want?

And where the FUCK are your millions already?! ;)

You might say I was kind of impatient with wanting success to just FIND me. To this day it's a trait I've often questioned within myself - this insatiable need for MORE, this inability to ever just stop, this DRIVE to keep. on. pushing - but ultimately it's a trait I've come to love about me, because hey-If you were already happy and had achieved, done, created 'enough' then why keep going at all? For me, happiness and my greatest fulfilment comes from the push for more and I know I will NEVER be done. It's kind of exciting even though it can certainly also be infuriating, not just for me but DEFINITELY for those around me who've been waiting years for me to be done and to just 'stick to something already' ... good luck waiting for that one honey! :)

But if you think about it...

And I'm sure if you stop and look back at your own journey...

45

And even though you might be just as impatient if not more so than me about your success...

Isn't it true that for somebody so damn impatient and biting at the bit, you've certainly done a pretty good job at putting the work in day in and day out even though you haven't yet got to where you want to be and even though, considering the drive for MORE, you perhaps NEVER WILL GET TO WHERE YOU WANT TO BE.

It's kind of weird actually.

And definitely a little crazy ... no wonder your friends and family have no freaking clue what you do let alone why!

But also -

It is AWESOME.

If I look back over the past 7 years+ online, for somebody so damn impatient and eager for more, I've done a pretty good job of waiting things out.

Paying my dues.

And just. keeping. on. going.

And that's the thing, isn't it?

If you look at my story, if you look at your own story, if you look at the story of anybody who has "made it"...

It's never about that one big thing, is it?

I spent so much time and energy - and perhaps you can relate - trying to figure out how to 'crack this thing', with the right product, the right launch, the right sales process. Working my butt off trying to emulate the work of those who I looked up to, trying to figure it OUT.

But it was never about figuring it out.

It was never about finding that magic bullet approach.

It was never about what I was MISSING for God's sakes!

And it was always, always, always, about just one thing.

Action.

Something.

Even when -

I didn't know how.

Or why.

Or whether I really was certifiable.

And even though I couldn't - most of the time! - CONNECT that action into the big visions and dreams I had for my life.

They say that imperfect action is the way forward. But I believe and I've found that if you take ANY action daily, and you actually DO SO DAILY, towards your biggest goals and dreams and 'one days', that that indeed and in its most simple state, is actually completely perfect PERFECT action.

Because action, drives you forward.

And action? It creates more action.

ACTION creates a HABIT of action.

It turns you into that person who continues to TAKE IT 'even though', and 'even when'.

I'm writing this right now from snowy Montana, just outside of Yellowstone National Park (where Yogi Bear lives, I think!). We're on a 3-week RV trip coast to coast across the US ... through Winter ... it's month thirteen on our laptop life journey ... our 14th country ... I now make over 100k a month all online and doing what I love ... my books are international best-sellers ... I am COMPLETELY living my dream (although never done!) and it really is at times UNBELIEVABLE when I think of all I've created but if I look back and really try to figure out how I brought all of this to life?

It's really, really simple.

I just kept going.

The ball rolled slowly for a long while.

Stopped and started even after it did kick off.

Went bloody backwards at top speed for a good period of time (think: over 100k debt and nearly choosing bankruptcy!)

But ultimately, and no matter what was going on with my income, my reach, my so-called success, the only constant, the only thing I kept doing was to just keep GOING.

Even now, as I continue to dream bigger than big and once again wonder if I'm crazy with the goals and dreams I have, I spend far less time worrying about the how than I spend just doing SOMETHING.

And ultimately, you could take it all away from me right now and return me to my tiny flat in Melbourne working full-time as a personal trainer and wondering how I'd ever become anything, and even though it might piss me off to lose all I've created, to be honest, my reaction?

Would be to pick myself up, get over it, and just keep going.

Because I have a message.

I have something to say ... a lot of it in fact!

I have a calling.

And I believe.

And I've learned that this stuff? When you build your business and your life around it? Is like a gazillion or so times more powerful than worrying about what you're missing, what strategy or approach you don't yet know about, what you 'should' be doing and DEFINITELY a lot more powerful than giving a fuck about what anybody else might be doing.

This is why I look at the 'latest and greatest' of the business world and of online sales and marketing tricks and strategies, and yes I'll admit it even at the online stars of the moment, and mostly it doesn't grab my attention.

Not because it COULDN'T ... I can be as prey to comparison and 'not being good enough' or 'not knowing enough' as the best of them! ... but because I've LEARNED -

It really doesn't matter.

At all.

What anybody else is doing.

Achieving.

Raving on about.

Caught up in.

Or what the latest rules are.

And I have to say I'm so freaking grateful I came online before the current wave of female entrepreneurs ... I think the unspoken and spoken rules of that world have a lot to answer for in terms of making the entire thing so much more complex than it really has to be ... never mind in terms of selling a message that success comes from following an approach rather than from being a certain type of person ... but that's a book for another day ;) ... what I see come out of this world is mostly indecision, confusion, comparison, and a helluva lot of wasted time and money ...

Because the truth is that if we all just stopped trying to figure it out -

And stopped trying to ask how -

Or why -

And stopped worrying at ALL what the rest of the world was up to or might think -

And just got the fuck on with it! -

We'd have a whole new wave of online millionaires, living with passion and purpose and from a place of flow, in just about no time at all.

If you would have told me, back in 2007, that I'd spend hundreds of thousands of dollars well before I ever made 'em, that I'd take 3 years to even really START getting anywhere, that I'd end up going BACKWARDS and nearly crashing and burning just when I thought I was 'getting there', that I'd 'waste' literally thousands of hours moving forward but yet not GETTING there, and that even when I WAS there - now - I'd still not be satisfied, well -

I think you know what I would have done.

Maybe tried to find a faster way.

Maybe 'wasted' even more time and money doing so.

But ultimately known that none of it, NONE of it, is wasted, when it moves you forward.

And ultimately known that it really doesn't matter what I know or who I know or how I do things so long as I just. keep. going.

Today, tomorrow, and every day after.

The truth is, and we so often forget this in our quest to figure it out and do things RIGHT, that whatever you can do, whatever you can dream, whatever you can imagine, is possible.

But for it to happen? YOU have to happen.

You have to begin.

And you have to start now, no matter what and no matter how.

The path to success is, quite simply, the path of she who takes action. Goethe, who I was reading this morning, and who I suppose knew a thing or two, said that bold action has genius, magic and power in it but that you have to begin it NOW. It's certainly worked for me :)

CHAPTER SIX - THE 100K A MONTH FORMULA

Let's make this real nice and simple.

You want a formula to make the BIG bucks, and do it fast?

I'll tell you how it goes.

I'll also tell you upfront - you might want to throw things at me after reading this. The truth hurts sometimes!

You ready?

Here we go -

Step 1.

Be you.

Step 2.

Let the world know.

Step 3.

Ask for money in exchange.

I guess there are a FEW more details that go into it, but seriously honey? You can take your money making strategy including ANYTHING I have ever taught you or written for you and tell it to go fuck itself.

Because this? THIS is the shit.

But let's lay it on down so we can see HOW it works.

Step 1 - Be You.

First things first. Ain't NOBODY going to be paying you money for ANYTHING if you're not abso-freaking-lutely and awesomely operating from a place of truth, alignment, and authenticity. I mean SURE ... you can find ways to hustle up a little or even a lot by operating OUT of alignment but it doesn't last, it doesn't create TRUE and WHOLE wealth, and all of that aside why the heck would you want to make money on any terms but your TRUE terms?

So when you think about how to craft your message, your service, your gifts to the world the VERY first and indeed the ONLY thing you need to ask to begin with is how you can tap into the true genius you have to share with the world.

Now if you want to talk NUMBERS, we can do that.

Take my business. Currently I'm consistently doing over 100k a month in revenue. By the time you read this who the heck knows where I'll be at. I'm aiming for over 10 million total revenue next year, so think big!

If we break it down -

Around 35k a month comes from payments for my Society of Women Who Dream Big and Make Shit Happen (my 1-year Mastermind).

Around 15-20k a month from my 8-week private mentoring, the Business Smackdown Intensive.

Around 10k a month from ongoing payments for my Rich Chick Coaching Certification.

Around 30k a month from whatever my launch of the month is, such as this month it was my 6-week It's Only Money Honey Program.

About 5-10k from random / miscellaneous – e.g. if I do a mini flash sale, or people just buying stuff off my site.

Around 5k a month from unsolicited one off coaching sessions.

But here's the thing. It's not like THAT is a breakdown of how your 100k months should look and it's certainly not a breakdown of what I expect my months to look like as time keeps ticking on. I know that my Society, for example, will eventually be bringing me by itself well over 100k a month. I also know that I rarely stop creating and promoting, so there'll be new things to add into the mix with each month that passes, some of which may flop and others which will go OFF and could also create their own 100k+ monthly revenue streams. And as for that 10 million per year goal (for starters!), well I have no IDEA where on earth that will come from!

And I don't really CARE, because what I know to be true about achieving a money goal, ANY money goal is that it's the INTENT and the ALIGNMENT that matters, not the process.

So as soon as you start looking at MY process, or anybody else's, or trying to come up with your OWN perfect process, you set yourself up for failure.

Repeat after me -

It is the OUTCOME I desire and intend to see happen, the way that I GET there is irrelevant SO LONG AS IT IS ALIGNED.

Do you see what I'm saying? If you want to set yourself up for true and MASSIVE wealth, whether it's 100k a month or 100k a DAY, then the ONLY thing you need to worry about is who you really want to be and how you can serve and create from that place.

From there it really is a relatively straightforward matter of setting yourself a crazy-ass big goal and then marching confidently forward, TRUSTING THAT BECAUSE YOU INTEND IT AND WHEN YOU REMAIN ALIGNED YOU WILL GET THERE.

And if you're me, you'll then set NEW goals to knock over the old ones well before you even reach those old ones :) personally I have NEVER hit a money goal as I always surpass it with a new goal before I get there!

Step 2 - Let the World Know

This is where we -

Market -

And sell -

And brand -

And generate LEADS -

And all that fun stuff.

But really? It's where we get the fuck over ourselves and just start putting shit out there. Like, fast. And, imperfectly. And, without worrying too much about the 'how' behind the putting out of it.

Here's the truth about SELLING, my sweet soul sister -

Selling? Is just telling people how you can help.

They have a need.

You understand.

And you can help.

So you tell them! And if they want it? They buy it! Which we'll talk about in the next step.

It's pretty darn simple and yet we complicate it SO much. Because really, you don't have to worry about how your sales PROCESSES look or whether you're doing what ALL the cool gals are doing when it comes to growing your list so long as you're just showing up every day and being AWESOMELY you, and you're in some way letting people KNOW about it every day.

So how do you let people know?

I guess it's true that the 'build it and they will come' philosophy doesn't really work SUPER well in the online space, although it does apply the longer you've been rolling that ball.

Until you get to 'fame level', here is what I suggest -

a) Know your message (be you!)

b) SHARE your message every day in some way. This could be blogging, video blogging, podcasting, running a free online training, sending out a special report, even a great social media update works. The KEY is that when you do any or all of this stuff you're actually sharing your TRUE and NO B.S. message. You know ... the stuff that makes people sit up and pay attention, and want more? THAT shit'll sell the pants off the VERY best sales strategy in the world, and without you even really trying. Trust me ... being you and letting the world hear that awesomeness is the FASTEST fast track to wealth.

c) LEVERAGE that message as best you can. You don't have to write a new blog every day ... you don't have to CREATE every day ... although most of us types are hard pressed not to! ... But you DO have to actively get the good word out every day. So share it. Re-post it. Email it. Ask others to share it. Start a conversation around it. Create yourself a little checklist of everything you can do each time you create a great message, to get the word out. THIS is something I didn't do for the first SEVEN FREAKING YEARS of being online and I would estimate it cost me a LOT of reach and a LOT of money. If you're going to have a message and you're going to get it out there then take the time to ACTUALLY GET IT OUT THERE.

d) Set it up so that you have at least one great message that people have to leave their email and name for in order to receive. Make it a REALLY good 'un. This is how you grow your list. Every day, check in on how that's going. Adjust if needed.

e) Repeat.

CONSISTENCY is a must. Where most entrepreneurs get it wrong is they are consistently INCONSISTENT with doing the work that actually matters. Which is bullshit, really, since the EFFECTIVE work is usually the easiest, the most fun, and the most 'flow' for you. Since it's about being you and all! I guess that's also why we RESIST it though, and often look for ways to complicate this thing that is business.

It really doesn't have to be more simple than being you, letting people know about it, and then, of course, you need to -

Step 3 - Ask for Money in Exchange

Another area where we get it OH so wrong. I often tell the story of how I didn't really make any money in my online business for my first 3 years online. Sometimes I include the reason -

I didn't really ASK for any money in the first 3 years online. Oh sure ... I released my first eBook (after 26 months!)... I ran an online course ... one in 3 years! And I made a LOT of plans.

Let me ask you something -

Is it possible? Just POSSible. That all of your planning and dreaming and mapping out is getting in the way of you actually DOING shit?

Repeat after me -

If I don't ask for money...

And I don't do so EVERY day...

Then I am HIGHLY unlikely to get paid!

I know.

You are WELCOME.

So how do you ask for money?

a) First, you need to have good valuable stuff that is WORTHY of money. THIS DOES NOT MEAN TAKE 6 MONTHS TO GO FIGURE OUT HOW TO CREATE THAT SHIT. Understand that when you are just being YOU, and sharing your true message that you know can HELP people, that THAT is of value. Of course you need to find a way to be able to pass it on such that people SEE the value in it and can benefit and be transformed by it. But if you take more than a day or two to do that? You're kidding yourself. You either know your stuff, or you don't. If you don't, then do some stuff you know.

b) Put together an offer. Again - NOT a license to take 6 months or even 6 weeks. Honestly you don't even need 6 DAYS to put together your next offer, and that's true even if right now you're at square one. Again - get the fuck over yourself and start making the shit happen that you SAY you want to make happen. If your life depended upon it, do you think you could come up with an offer in the next 6 HOURS? Okay then. An offer could be coaching or teaching or an online course or a Bootcamp or an event or a workshop or anything really. It's just you, sharing how you can help. In a way that helps people.

c)   TELL them about the offer. Put it in your blogs, your podcasts, and your videos. Put it on social media. Make ads for it, if you like. Have a sales page. Run a launch party! Give a free training and then make a SPECIAL offer on that offer, which only lasts for a while, so that people are compelled to take it NOW if they want it at all.

d)   Repeat.

CONSISTENCY, remember?

So in this area - asking for money is not something you do once every so often with a big fanfare because hey! It's a launch! It's a promotion! It's a sale! Something you may or may not know about businesses? They SELL stuff. And how OFTEN do they sell stuff? Well GENERALLY about as often as they're open. So by all means ... if you really want ... work

365 days a year and sell for only a week at a time 3x a year when you 'launch' ... I'm not saying that can't work ... there are some good examples out there of people who launch only ONCE a year ... but it's not the way I roll and so it's not what I'm gonna teach. I say -

Sell the SHIT out of your shit every damn day of every damn week. Ad infinITUM.

How best to do this? It is NOT by hustling your butt off every day. Instead, think systems. Think LEVERAGE. Take the stuff you've been sharing and selling. Set it up so that new people who are joining your list get told about it automatically. Add to this process with MORE free value and MORE offers as you create both.

That's it baby.

The 100k a month, a day, a MINUTE formula. The actual number? Will be whatever you intend and then consciously set out to ALLOW and create. The details of GETTING there? Are exactly what we just outlined, so for the love of God commit to FOLLOWING those details ... consistently ... always, consistently.

So let's recap.

1. Be YOU, be TRUE, and know your message.

2. SHARE that stuff, no holds barred and with ABSOLUTE truth.

(Including: requiring people to hand over their email in exchange for some of your BEST work)

3. Ask for money and set up automatic processes around this as you go.

4. A gazillion. Repeat, adjust, repeat, but ALWAYS take action daily.

Cool? Let's move on.

CHAPTER SEVEN - THE MONEY-MAKING MESSAGE

This message thing? It's kinda essential. And you've seen me harp on about it enough to know that.

What I know about YOU, is that if you're like I was for oh so long or if you're like so many of my clients are, you feel ... uncertain. About whether you really know your message at all. About whether it even matters! About whether anybody cares. And definitely about whether anyone would PAY to hear it, or how you could actually package it for them.

I used to think that a lot of people struggled to really know what their true message, or calling was. Over time I realised

I was wrong. You already know your message. You know your calling. You damn sure know your purpose.

You just don't know how to live it, never mind profit from it.

I hope I'm wrong of course!

But this is what I've found to be true.

Now if you don't KNOW that you know your message already, let me tell you -

You so do. You've got it. You know it. It's there. It's there in your old journals, the same desires and dreams and beliefs written time and again and then pushed away, ignored, resisted. It's there in the coaching sessions you've had over the years, discussed, played around with, painfully come back to and then once again shelved. It's there in your mind, where it's always been. In your heart, where it longs to thrive. And in your soul, where it forms the very core of you.

Don't you see?

Your message is YOU. It's the essence of your beliefs and your values and your musts and your very YOUness.

So let's just admit, and agree, together-

You know your message.

But ah, the living of it, that really IS the thing to talk about now, isn't it?

How do you speak your TRUTH when people just want the boring surface shit they think they need?

How do you say what you REALLY think when you'll likely be judged for it, hated, or at least not be part of the tribe?

How do you STAKE A CLAIM ON BEING YOU when the world just wants another lemming it can feel safe and secure with?

It's simple -

You just do.

Even though yes, they will, and no, you won't (and that's okay).

And you just do.

Where I suppose we can get a LITTLE bit strategic about it is to recognise that if people don't GET your message then it's not your job to try and MAKE them get it by virtue of force.

In this situation, which is common - you, you have a deeper message to share and they, they just want to know the nuts and bolts stuff that you're SO over - you have two choices.

1. Change your audience to people who DO already get it. The thing to realise is that those people either still ALSO want the flashy, the catchy, the nuts and bolts of it all or if they don't then they ARE you and therefore might not NEED you.

2. Speak the language of those you are speaking to. This means you TALK about the rapid weight loss, or secrets to making money, or explosive ways to grow your business, or whatever it might be that THEY are looking for. You use that as the 'hook' to share your message. And then you speak about whatever you want to speak about. You share the TRUTH. Which may not be what they expected. Just like what I'm sharing in this book, perhaps, may not be what you expected from the title. But would you have bought it, had I titled it "How to Have an Aligned Business and Life"? If yes, you're a diehard fan and I thank you :)

You have to understand that for you to stand out and allow your message to come to LIGHT, you need to be able to get people's attention. Otherwise, how can you share to them? The fastest way to get people's attention? Honour where they are at and meet them there. You get to have YOUR journey, so let them have theirs.

But really, that's the easy part. Speaking the language of your people. The tougher part is allowing yourself to believe that you can and also SHOULD speak the language of YOU when it comes to your delivery.

That you can write about what you really want to write about.

Talk about what you really want to talk about.

Teach THAT.

HELP people with that.

Be the GURU of that, and proud of it.

Rather than doing the stuff you think you have to do to stand out, get noticed, and make some money.

And do it all gloves off.

The TRUTH is that you will never create wealth - not 100k a month or ANY other number you might choose - from a place of the wrong service.

You were born to serve in a certain way.

You were born to show up as you.

You're NEVER going to be satisfied when you ignore that calling.

So you might as well start now.

Not sure how to live your message?

You're complicating it.

You live your message by living your message.

A 'trick', if you'd like one, to help you be able to SEE it, is to think about how your life would look and who you would be if you were ALREADY living as that person.

And then act as if.

One life baby. Time to press play!

CHAPTER EIGHT - STEP IT UP WARRIOR PRINCESS!

This thing we call life? What we need to realise is that it's already happening.

And I know -

First place in the Stating the Obvious competition, right?

But there's a difference between KNOWING something, and DOING something. In the same way that common sense? Is not common practice. So let me ask you -

(I do like to ask stuff!)

- Do you make it a common practice to press play every day?

Pressing play is -

Going all out.

Towards your dreams.

Taking imperfect action, daily.

Even when you don't know how.

Trusting in the process.

Being committed to the PRACTICE not the result you think you 'have to have'.

Facing fear in the eye and then telling it to get the fuck out of your way.

To press play, you must be a warrior.

You have to have already faced and fought and overcome the battle that is being true to yourself.

You must have invested the hours, yes, but more importantly you must have invested YOU. Your essence, your energy, your emotion, your very soul.

You must have stared into the eye of the beast and then gone forth ANYWAY.

This means -

You did not flinch at trouble.

You did not allow torment to instruct you.

You did not allow your DESTINY to be dictated by your emotions.

Instead, what you did, and even though perhaps you veered off the path many times over, was to just. keep. going.

Trusting in the TRUTH that you? Do have a calling. And you're allowed to live it.

When your ultimate belief is that you CAN do it, and then you choose to ALLOW it, you can continue through whatever you have to. You are relentless. You are unstoppable. You will NEVER quit. The end will be your death, and that's just how it is.

So if that's what pressing play is, let me ask you again -

Are you doing it?

Truly?

And all out?

And CONSISTENTLY?

Is the practice of you creating your dream business, your dream life, your YOU, one that you ACTUALLY practice?

Or is it a sometimes / maybe / when you're able or know how sort of a thing?

If the latter is the case, congratulations -

You're part of the tribe. You're with the majority. You are normal. You are SAFE.

And you are already dead.

It's okay if you're not QUITE in the practice you must be. It's how we are, as warriors in the making. Teetering on the edge, waiting to jump. Hoping, perhaps, that somebody will push us.

Of course when I say it's okay it's ONLY okay if a) you're aware of it and b) you intend to do something about it - now.

Because here's the thing about BIG success -

It's not about finding the right path, it's not about the right APPROACH that you just haven't figured out yet. If you picked up this book looking for a formula in the TRADITIONAL sense, a fill-in-the-gaps or join-the-dots sort of thing then guess what? It doesn't exist.

So if there is no step-by-step formula, no magic solution, no path you just HAVE to find, then what is there?

Step One. (be you)

Step Two. (share it)

Step Three. (receive value in exchange)

But do you remember what came after all of these steps?

REPEAT. Be CONSISTENT.

That's what stepping it up means. That's what pressing play is about. That's what being a WARRIOR is.

Go do it princess. Commit to excellence. Commit to the PRACTICE. Commit to ETERNITY at this thing. Commit, ultimately, to you.

CHAPTER NINE - HOW TO FUCK IT ALL UP

Something I learned, once I finally allowed money to flow to me and business and life to be easy and straightforward, was just how tough I had made it on myself over the years.

You might have heard people say that making money or achieving even the biggest dreams and goals can be easy, and fun. It's true! Of course that doesn't mean it won't also be hard work, but let's face it - you're already working hard anyway! Might as well do it in a way that works FOR you.

The greatest block to you creating the money, the business, the life, all of it, is not that you don't know what to do or how to get there. The greatest block, and the one you'll have to battle on a near daily basis, is you.

YOU are the one who will determine whether or not you take action every day, in spite of all the, often very valid, reasons you maybe can't.

YOU are the one who will choose to press on, or be swayed.

YOU are the one who must pick yourself up as many times as it takes, and then 1000 more.

YOU are the one who must be bloodied, torn apart, ripped in two, on your journey, and then continue fighting REGARDLESS.

It is all. down. to. YOU.

And the very GREATEST challenge you will face, is not only realising and ACKNOWLEDGING this responsibility but then also crafting your days accordingly.

Because the danger - the very real and present danger - is that somewhere on your road to living your dreams and having it all you get distracted by something close enough to deceive you, yet never enough to satisfy you.

This is the writer who ends up spending her time on coaching, and crams her craft in to 20 minutes here and there.

It's the speaker born to impact millions, who accepts an hourly fee for her services.

It's the creator swept up in administrative tasks, and Facebook, and email.

It's the leader who is busy teaching.

It's the warrior who spends her days answering to others.

It's the you who allows the true genius you were brought here to share to be dulled, dimmed and destroyed by the mundanity of Getting Shit Done.

This is the REALITY of how most people allow their destiny to be carved. Simply, they don't. They play along the sidelines of their own life, desperate to get into the ring but yet ready and armed with a bevy of excuses when their turn is offered.

NOW is the time when you need to be honest with yourself about whether YOU are living on the sidelines of your own life.

NOW is the only time you have and you have NO more time left to live the wrong life.

NEAR enough is NOT good enough.

And there is nothing - no NOTHING - not money, not fame, not so-called security, that can compensate you for never quite living your dreams, never quite going all out, never REALLY seeing where you can go. And never fully being you.

So now.

Let's commit.

You and me.

That this? THIS HAS GOT TO STOP.

NO more putting off for another NEVER what you've been BURNING TO DO AND BE FOR ETERNITY.

You will never, ever, EVER forgive yourself.

Do you realise how serious this shit is?

Just because you HAVE a purpose does NOT mean you will live it. YOU have to choose. You HAVE to choose. You have to CHOOSE.

And you have to rip that motherfucker of a Band-Aid off now.

How do you do that?

It's very simple, it's far more straightforward than perhaps you'd like, and you can do it in just a few moments. Yes. No more fucking around. No more excuses. I'm not buying them and NEITHER ARE YOU.

Here's what we do.

Very quickly, a list. A list of everything that comes to mind that you currently spend your time on. Start with your business activities, and then do the same for your life.

For me, the list might look something like this -

Writing and planning and journaling and visioning and answering emails and speaking with my staff and marketing and selling and speaking and coaching and running events and reading new advice and writing copy and creating new content and learning new skills and keeping up in my forums and so on.

What's yours look like?

Now, time for brutal truth.

On your list: What would you keep if you knew you had that hundred million dollars in the bank, you were in a position of being able to do whatever you like for the rest of FOREVER, and you had a team of servile minions who would get EVERYTHING else done for you.

Quickly, now! WHAT WOULD YOU KEEP?

THAT is the work you are really here to do.

For me - writing and speaking. From the heart. From flow. No preparation. Just letting the muse deliver.

That's it.

What's yours? Has it even made it onto your list of current activities? And if it has, what percentage of your time do you spend on it?

80%?

Not freaking likely, because if you did you'd be too busy printing money to read this book.

50%?

I doubt it.

The very vast majority of entrepreneurs reading this book will be lucky to spend 5-10% of their working time doing the real work they are called to do. If you're more than that, great. But if it's NOT at 80% then you've got some changes to make. And I trust you can identify what the real 'formula' you need here is.

Yes?

So, a commitment.

A commitment to excellence.

To consistency.

To showing up every day in those areas but more importantly of all to showing up relevant to the WORK YOU ARE HERE TO DO in those areas.

80% is your minimum darling.

Don't know how to make that happen, how it can possibly be realistic, how you can keep all your other balls in the air?

Let 'em fall.

It's the only way.

YES it will be messy and YES it will cause chaos and YES it will hurt. Nobody said that crafting your dreams is neat and tidy and will put a smile on the faces of everybody you encounter.

But if it puts a smile on yours, isn't that what matters?

Face the mess, or you'll instead become one.

And for God's sakes -

Get out of your own way.

CHAPTER TEN - WHERE THE RUBBER HITS THE ROAD

You can read a book like this, and be so easily and enthusiastically inspired.

Yes! You think to yourself.

I WILL do that. I'm going to DO it! I'm going to finally BE THE ME I WAS BORN TO BE!

I can't wait!

It'll be awesome!

It's going to ROCK!

I'm going to CHANGE THE WORLD.

Just let me finish off this ONE tiny thing...

And, DEATH.

THAT, my delusional darling, is how you kill your dreams. Been there, got the t-shirt and I can tell you that it is NOT worth it.

Get the fuck over EVERYTHING you think you have to do if it is not in fact LIVING THE LIFE YOU WERE BORN FOR.

Do you hear me?

THIS IS LIFE AND DEATH.

Success is a BATTLE, and it's one that few will face. ONLY the true warriors survive. So let me ask you, and what you answer you must LIVE FOR -

ARE YOU A WARRIOR OR ARE YOU A WANNABE?

There's no in between.

There is no finishing off of things.

The battle has already begun.

And you're being left behind already.

Every so often, someone will read one of my books and message me excitedly about how pumped up they are and how excited to take action.

I'm DOING it, Kat! This is HAPPENING!

I get excited for THEM. And then I see -

I can't start today, I'm so tired. But I'm starting tomorrow, I promise!

The fuck. you. will.

It's now or NEVER baby. You don't start the race that's already begun when you freaking FEEL like it.

You start now. You pick up your tired and weary and scared ass and you GET TO FUCKING WORK.

Or you quit wasting my time, and your breath.

So go.

Go now.

And continue going on.

The battle's already begun, but the race?

It never ends.

Remember -

Life is Now. Press Play.

Kat x

EXTRACT FROM THE PUSH: THE RICH CHICKS GUIDE TO BEING MOTHER-FUCKING EXCEPTIONAL, A SUPERWOMAN, THE 1%, AND OKAY WITH IT

Grab Your Copy On Amazon Today

Introduction

The push is about that constant need to be, to do, to prove yourself.

No matter how much you do, it's never enough.

No matter how high of a mountain you scale - and even though you may feel good about it, for a moment! - there's still more ahead of you.

An unquenchable thirst for -

What?

To show the world that you are an achiever, a go-getter, a superwoman?

To position yourself as a leader, a winner, the best?

No.

The admiration of others is nice, to be sure. But to be honest it's also just expected.

You KNOW you do more.

You KNOW you take on "too much", and yet still complete it.

You KNOW that the way you live your life is not only 'impressive', but in fact astonishing, astounding and even plain unbelievable to others.

You KNOW you are the 1% within the 1% within the 1%.

So really, what is there to prove? Proving you're ahead of the rest proves nothing to the one person that counts.

Which brings us back to the push.

The push is not about the world.

The world and the limitations of the ordinary person, yes even the 'successful' ordinary person, really have nothing to do with you.

Because the push is about you.

The push is about your need to prove something to YOU.

The PROBLEM with the push and the way you dance with it now, is that you're trying to prove the unprovable.

Another way to look at it - haven't you ALREADY proven (and how many times now, let's be honest?) that no matter what you may do, will ever do, could ever do, no matter how many times you achieve the improbable or even the impossible it will still. never. be. enough.

And the push will always win because the only thing that truly IS impossible, for you, is to not push.

So why this book?

It's simple. If you don't learn how to work WITH the push, the push will control you, forever torment you, and very easily can, through the exhausting search for MORE, destroy you.

This book is about taking charge of the push.

Using it for good.

Using it to be, and do, and have what you TRULY desire and are born for, rather than having it TELL you what you need to be, and do, and have, in order to be ENOUGH.

Know right now that you are already enough but also you will never BE enough, and that's okay. In fact, it's more than okay. Because the realisation that the end of achievement never comes is incredibly freeing, and if you really THINK about it, it allows you to now move forward from a place of only giving a fuck about the things you really do give a fuck about.

The secret is - you have to know what those things are, and you have to be able to take CHARGE of the push and make it dance to your tune.

What this book is really about, is finding your own tune. And then spinning the world on its head as you dance the motherfreaking crap out of it.

Chapter One - Sometimes You Just Wanna Be Normal!

There was this song that used to run through my head over and over, as a little girl. It was still there as a teenager, and sometimes it still comes from nowhere; surprises me. I believe it's from the musical "Fiddler on the Roof" -

"If I were a rich man, la-di-da-di-da-di-da-di-da-da-dah .... I'd travel all around, if I were a wealthy MAN! I wouldn't have to work hard, la-di-da-di-da-di-da-di-da-da-dah.... I'd (something) all the day, if I were a wealthy MAN!"

A catchy tune for sure, but I think the real reason it has stuck with me for some 20+ years now is that deep within me I always knew -

Well, yes, what if you WERE rich Katrina?

What if you DID have it all?

What if you could do ANYTHING, BE anything, and change the world?

What then?

Let me pose the same question to you-

What if you WERE "truly" rich, as far as your eye could see you had already reached...?

What if you DID have it all...?

What if you HAD done it all...?

Then what?

And the answer is as certain within you as it is within me -

More.

And begin again.

For you know as well as I do - there always is more. You can reach as far as you can see. You CAN do anything, be anything, have it all, but when you get there there will still. be. more.

And to tell the truth? It's fucking exhausting almost as much as it is exhilarating, ain't it? And sometimes, as you look around you at everyone going about whatever it is the normal person goes about, you have this thought, for a moment, of how it must feel to live a life in which one clocks on and then clocks off and is HAPPY. A life where all that matters is the stability of a home, a set income likely not enough but perfectly acceptable, good food and drink, a family and friends, the obligatory travel and various others accoutrements of a 'successful' life.

And you wonder, for a moment, at how freeing it must be to be able to reach the end of your work day and be done.

To feel relaxed and sufficient in the idea of spending your evenings or weekends watching TV, reading magazines, following the news or sports, or just 'hanging out'.

And you imagine, for a moment, an alternative life where you too feel so free, so complete, so secure, and what a RELIEF it might be to rid yourself of this constant 'damned if you do and damned if you don't' pressure that for the LIFE of you you don't know if you'll ever release.

Hint: you won't.

And: wake the fuck up beautiful because the truth, that you already know, is that the apparent freedom of the normal woman is the furthest possible thing from freedom that could ever exist, for freedom and also SECURITY has nothing to do with how you spend your time and nor does it have anything to do with where you are or with knowing what to expect from your income, your home, your family, yourself. And it has everything to do with how you see the world and how you see what is possible for you.

So if we're going to do this, let's really do it, yes?

Let's have the goddamn self-respect to be HONEST about what you really want...

Who you truly are...

And how it all needs to play out for you...

And the truth, of course, is that you never really COULD do normal, could you?

Oh sure, perhaps you tried. A little. Or as best as it ever could be possible for you to try, really. In the same sort of way that a cat might try to pretend it's a dog. You can mimic and learn and study and APPLY yourself but at the end of the day it really doesn't matter what you do nor how you do it, normal just ain't your thing.

AND YOU'RE GLAD FOR IT.

Which is an understatement, but you get the point.

And you know what else? As much as you might IMAGINE what it would be like to lead the normal life, to be THAT girl, the reality of even the IDEA of it horrifies you so much that you really find it very, very difficult to believe that ANYBODY could be happy that way.

Are they really?

Is it possible?!

You know what?

Who cares?! This is about you! And what YOU need right now is to stand up straight, grit your teeth, throw your shoulders back and your chest out and finally learn to CLAIM your awesomeness. And then embrace what it MEANS to be so goddamn awesome, what ALL of it means.

PUSH: From now on, let's agree - you are awesome, no wait! You are freaking EXCEPTIONAL. Mother FUCKING exceptional, no less. And you're okay with it, so the world and it's seduction of 'slow down', and 'relax', can really just go screw itself. There's WORK to be done, and in the best possible way.

Click here to order your copy

SO WHAT NOW?

As a thank-you for reading my book I'd like to invite you to join me in a FREE 8 Day Video Training Series I've created on The Truth About Successful Manifestation!

You can sign up right now and you'll have Day 1 in your inbox immediately!

www.thekatrinaruthshow.com/manifestationfreecourse

The Truth About Successful Manifestation

A Free 8-Day Online Course with Katrina Ruth to get you UNDERSTANDING ... ACTING ON ... CLEARING THE STUFF in the way of ... and DOING THE FREAKIN' work to manifest SUCCESSFULLY.

You.

You're a rule-breaker, and you always have been.

That black sheep thang you've got going on? It's not that you even really TRIED to be a rebel, actually ... although you're not complaining about the fact that it does make you feel kinda cool

But no, you didn't set out to TEAR DOWN THE RULES, deconstruct the norms, REFUSE to say yes just because it's the 'done thing' or 'how it is'.

It just kind of ... happened.

Somewhere between growing up and doing the right thing and trying to fit in and TRYING desperately to be cool, accepted, validated, approved of, MADE worthy, the tide turned.

You started to ... notice things.

THINK about things.

And most of all, or so it's often seemed?

You started to reject things.

Such as the idea that there's a right or a wrong way to do life.

Such as the idea that being a good grown-up …
entrepreneur … creative … DRIVEN person … SUCCESSFUL person … requires you to be, well –

{You're okay with me just being straight up with you from the get go, right?? Cool …}

– Stepfordfuckingpreneur

Or person.

Either way.

Because let's face it baby –

You were NEVER gonna be able to do normal, were you? I mean SURE, you may have well TRIED, and indeed you did! I get it! That need to be LIKED runs deep. But in the end?

You were always going to give in to being you.

So,

If you're ready to say yes to YOU –

To being fully and UNAPOLOGETICALLY you –

And going ALL IN, at BEING you -

Then I'd like to share this gift with you.

The Truth About Successful Manifestation

An 8-Day Manifestation Video Series designed to get you UNDERSTANDING ... ACTING ON ... CLEARING THE STUFF in the way of ... and DOING THE FREAKIN' work to manifest SUCCESSFULLY.

Yes?

YES.

Join me here, now -

www.thekatrinaruthshow.com/manifestationfreecourse

Love for 'The Truth About Successful Manifestation'

'Thanks for the 8 day Successful Manifestation challenge!. I have so many things to work on. I was born into the wrong school of life, as you call it, but in my mind have always been in the right school.

Spent too much time listening to wrong thinking. Now getting realigned with who I've always been. Your challenge has been a great reminder to me of how to be'

- Gwen Finney

'I just wanted to share my absolute excitement and manifestation proof list! I actually got specific and gave it a timeline - my dream apartment was going to appear and be available for rent by the end of January.

On Tuesday I inspected an apartment that I absolutely fell in love with and KNEW I HAD to have. Today I've been pre-approved because I just submitted my application knowing it was done. In the face of all my conversations about not being 'employed' or being able to prove my income etc ... I'm putting it out and claiming that it's done and that I will be able to pay for it easily and in flow, every month'

- Liora Levin

'Oh my fucking god ..... manifesting is now my middle name!

Since the beginning of this year, I've stepped into manifesting my desired and dream life ... I am living the level of where I want to be before I get there and it's because I've manifested and aligned to my truest and highest level of being!

Everyday that Kat has come on with truths of manifestation, I've stepped in and gone deeper with my life and business plans and today I've had so many firecracker BOOM moments to show me that it's all about pressing play with the delicacy of healing, living and loving a millionaires' world!'

- Harmoni Shakti Dowling

'Hey I just wanted to say thank-you so much Katrina Ruth for doing this for us x

I've had a huge breakthrough with my money story already after doing this mindset work. To me now it is completely normal to be tripling my account day trading which happened on Friday after placing my very first trade in the currency market!!

I never trusted myself enough to make my own trading decisions until now … move over Warren Buffet here I come!!'

- Mieko Louise

'I manifested something HUGE into my life today that I think I had been hesitant to even ask the Universe for before watching the videos. I think I felt it was just impossible and could never happen for me. So, I journaled and found blocks in my thinking and journaled some more to figure out how to work them out and I think I am working through those blocks. I am so grateful for everything and feel totally at peace and fully aligned right now. It is an absolutely amazing feeling! THANK YOU KAT!'

- Jessica Anglin

'Today I've manifested everything I said I would over the last week!!!!

I got my date, my massage, my Internet is working today as I said it would, I have money coming back to me from (my) insurance company cleared by tomorrow, and I have connected with 2 coaches that offer training in the area I want.

Now for my next 10 features between Forbes, Fortune, Addicted2success, and the other 7 media outlets by the end of September. Watch me do it. I'm limitless.'

- Amanda Hines

'I manifested 2 NEW six-figure sponsors for my event!!!!!!!! A big take away has been that I have always been a big dreamer and I realised that deep down I sometimes think I dream too big. That has changed since being here!!!! Thank you Kat!!!!!!!!!!!!'

Laura Radford Garne

ABOUT THE AUTHOR, KATRINA RUTH (FORMERLY KAT LOTERZO)

Katrina Ruth (formerly Kat Loterzo) is an entrepreneur and writer based on Australia's sunny Gold Coast. When she isn't furiously unleashing her true message via her daily blog 'The Daily Asskickery', or her #PurposeChurchwithKat live videos, she is running her multi-million dollar online coaching business as an entertainer, speaker and success mentor to 'the crazy ones'.

With 50+ self-published books (mostly Amazon best sellers), over a decade in online business, and several hundred soul-led product and program launches under her belt, Katrina is known as a 'Content Queen' who just doesn't stop. She believes that you CAN have it all, on your terms, so long as you're willing to get honest with yourself about what you're really here to do in the world, and her great mission in life is to help you find who you are - and then become it.

Before transitioning into her current work Katrina initially built a 7-figure online fitness business by following zero of the 'rules' around internet marketing, and to this day her process includes the truth that YOU know best what is right for you and your audience. Now, as a mentor, she kicks the butts of the worlds top entrepreneurs, leaders, visionaries and creators and is arguably the most hardcore chick online.

Katrina lives with her 2 children in her dream home overlooking the ocean. She is obsessed with great coffee, great wifi, great wine and great training of the mind and body, as well as creating as much content as humanly possible on the topic of alignment and taking MASSIVE fucking action.

Katrina is also an <u>expert in "No B.S" coaching</u> and would love to help you create a business and life you love, completely on your terms!

Follow Kat here:

Facebook: www.facebook.com/lifeisnow.pressplay

Instagram: www.instagram.com/thekatrinaruthshow

YouTube: www.youtube.com/c/thekatrinaruthshow

Ebooks: https://www.booksforkickasswomen.com

Sign up for Katrina's FREE 8-Part Video Training Series - **'The Truth About Successful Manifestation'** at:

www.thekatrinaruthshow.com/manifestationfreecourse

MORE BOOKS FOR KICKASS ENTREPRENEURS

For more kickass books for kickass women (& men), including free downloads go to:

www.booksforkickasswomen.com

Also, don't forget to <u>follow me on Facebook</u>, to keep in touch and get access to my latest Blog Posts.

It would be my absolute honour and pleasure to have you in my community and give you the motivation, inspiration, education and butt-kickin' <u>empowerment</u> you need to get out there and create the business and life of your dreams!

I have to warn you though … my style is somewhat out there. I'm not gonna hold back on saying what I think. I may very well call you on your sh*t … often. And if I think you're limiting your ability to create what you WANT to create, and CAN create then I'll be coming down on you like a ton of bricks. Loving bricks, but still.

YOUR HELP PLEASE!

Did you enjoy this book, find it helpful, or love how it kicked your ass?

I'd love it if you could take two minutes of your time to leave a review for this book on Amazon, even if you purchased it direct from my website and not from Amazon.

Thank you so much!

And don't forget –

Life is Now. Press Play!

Kat x

Made in the USA
San Bernardino,
CA